Platypus and Fly

Fly is sneaky and very cheeky. He likes to tease and annoy other creatures around him. Then he meets Platypus, who is ready for lunch. The race is on, but who will win?

This picture book targets /l/ blends and is part of *Speech Bubbles 2*, a series of picture books that target specific speech sounds within the story.

The series can be used for children receiving speech therapy, for children who have a speech sound delay/disorder, or simply as an activity for children's speech sound development and/or phonological awareness. They are ideal for use by parents, teachers or caregivers.

Bright pictures and a fun story create an engaging activity perfect for sound awareness.

Picture books are sold individually, or in a pack. There are currently two packs available – *Speech Bubbles 1* and *Speech Bubbles 2.* Please see further titles in the series for stories targeting other speech sounds.

Melissa Palmer is a Speech Language Therapist. She worked for the Ministry of Education, Special Education in New Zealand from 2008 to 2013, with children aged primarily between 2 and 8 years of age. She also completed a diploma in children's writing in 2009, studying under author Janice Marriott, through the New Zealand Business Institute. Melissa has a passion for articulation and phonology, as well as writing and art, and has combined these two loves to create *Speech Bubbles*.

What's in the pack?

Platypus and Fly

Targeting /l/ Blends

Melissa Palmer

LONDON AND NEW YORK

First published 2021
by Routledge
2 Park Square, Milton Park, Abingdon, Oxon OX14 4RN

and by Routledge
52 Vanderbilt Avenue, New York, NY 10017

Routledge is an imprint of the Taylor & Francis Group, an informa business

British Library Cataloguing-in-Publication Data
A catalogue record for this book is available from the British Library

Library of Congress Cataloging-in-Publication Data
Names: Palmer, Melissa (Speech language therapist), author.
Title: Platypus and fly : targeting l blends / Melissa Palmer.
Description: Milton Park, Abingdon, Oxon ; New York, NY : Routledge, 2021. |
Series: Speech bubbles 2 Identifiers: LCCN 2020048789 (print) |
LCCN 2020048790 (ebook) | ISBN 9780367648879 (paperback) | ISBN 9781003126782 (ebook)
Subjects: LCSH: Speech therapy for children–Juvenile literature. | Speech therapy–Juvenile literature. |
Articulation disorders in children–Juvenile literature. | Flies–Juvenile literature.
Classification: LCC RJ496.S7 P325 2021 (print) | LCC RJ496.S7 (ebook) |
DDC 618.92/85506–dc23 LC record available at https://lccn.loc.gov/2020048789
LC ebook record available at https://lccn.loc.gov/2020048790

ISBN: 978-1-138-59784-6 (set)
ISBN: 978-0-367-64887-9 (pbk)
ISBN: 978-1-003-12678-2 (ebk)

Typeset in Calibri
by Newgen Publishing UK

Platypus and Fly

While skies are **bl**ue and sun is shining,

Platypus is a**sl**eep,

His fur all **sl**eek, his duck-like bill **gl**eams,

As he **sl**eeps by the river deep.

What’s that sound? **Pl**atypus hears a buzz,

Feels a **fl**apping near his ear,

-l-l-l-l-l-l-l-l-l-l-l-l-l-l-l-l-l-l-l-l-l-l-l-l-l-

He **sl**owly opens one eye – a tiny **sl**it,

To see what was **fl**ying there.

A **fl**y! A **fl**y! A tiny **bl**ack **fl**y

Was **fl**itting all around,

Playing as he **fl**apped his wings,

Spinning and landing on the ground.

With a scowl and a howl **Pl**atypus pounced,

Trying to grab **Fl**y with a **sl**ap,

But **Fl**y was too quick and **fl**ew out of the way,

Platypus’s paw landing with a **cl**ap.

Fly **sl**owly landed on a pretty **bl**ue **fl**ower,

Thinking he'd look just like a bee.

But **Pl**atypus was right behind him –

Fly had just enough time to **fl**ee.

Fly **fl**ew over the river,

Thinking he would be safe over there,

But **pl**atypuses are very good swimmers –

Fly didn't realise he was near!

Slap went **Pl**atypus's paw on the water,

Fly went tumbling under,

Snap snap snap went **Pl**atypus's beak.

To **Fl**y it sounded like thunder!

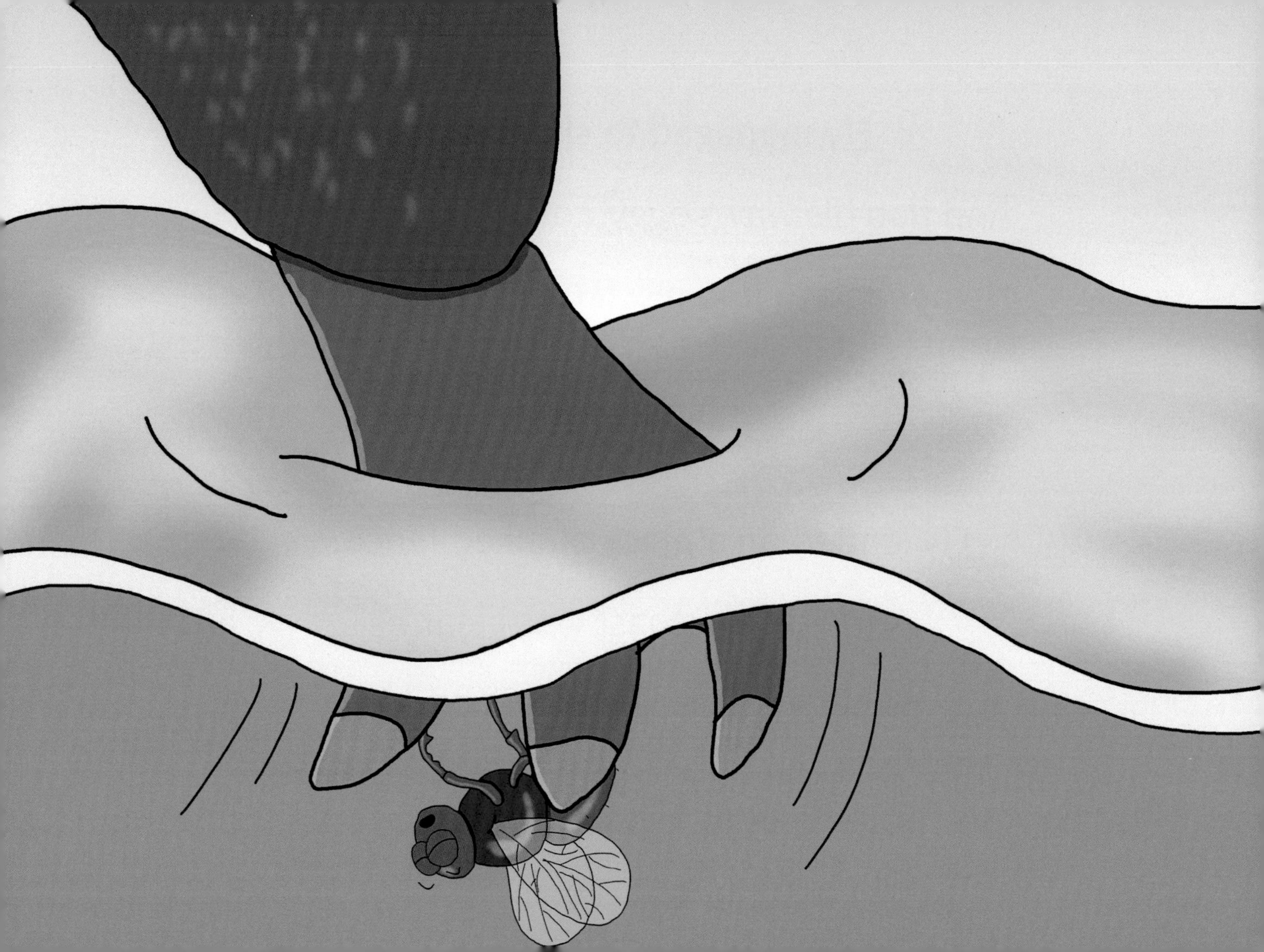

Fly managed to **sl**ip past,

And **fl**ap his way, soggy, to the riverbank.

He needed to find a safe **pl**ace to **cl**ean –

The water had made his wings so lank.

Fly landed on a **bl**ack **pl**anked fence,

Hoping the coast was **cl**ear.

He **cl**eaned his wings and body,

Still feeling full of fear.

Wings now **cl**ean, **Fl**y couldn't help

Feeling like the future was pretty **bl**eak.

He went to **fl**it away,

But froze when he spied **Pl**atypus's beak!

Silent and still, **Fl**y **cl**osed his eyes.

He waited for his fate.

He thought he would be **Pl**atypus's dinner,

A prize served on a **pl**ate.

But after a while **Fl**y opened his eyes

To find himself alone.

Platypus was gone, **Fl**y was free.

It was time for him to have **fl**own.

Fly realised that he was as **bl**ack as the **pl**ank,

So **Pl**atypus just didn't see

Where **Fl**y had been hiding in **pl**ain sight,

And now it was time to **fl**ee!

Fly **fl**itted off, now free to **pl**ay,

And **fl**ew in circles round a fern,

Then up, up and away, forever and a day,

Never to return.